Wilton's Wit For Children

By
Clyde Wilton

Compiled & Edited By
Aaron Z. Wilton

Order this book online at www.trafford.com
or email orders@trafford.com

Most Trafford titles are also available at major online book retailers.

Printed in the United States of America.

ISBN: 978-1-4669-0450-7 (sc)
ISBN: 978-1-4669-0452-1 (hc)
ISBN: 978-1-4669-0451-4 (e)

Library of Congress Control Number: 2011960891

Trafford rev. 11/16/2011

 www.trafford.com

North America & International
toll-free: 1 888 232 4444 (USA & Canada)
phone: 250 383 6864 ♦ fax: 812 355 4082

Preface

After working through two versions of my book, Wilton's Wit, which was first published in 2009, there were a number of friends who saw the value of transforming the original book intended for adults into a book for children. So, after completely revising the book, making it more suitable for children to appreciate and comprehend, this current work, Wilton's Wit For Children, has arisen.

At the time when I was growing up, in the 1920's and 1930's, there was a completely different emphasis on life. There were not the modern electronic wonders that today bring us news immediately from around the world. Instead, it took much longer to hear about major happenings such as earthquakes, hurricanes, wars, and other important events.

My world began on a small farm in North Texas, and our main communication about the events outside of our farm was through a party-line telephone, which only extended to relatives about three miles away. My first real fascination with electronic technology came with building crystal set radios, which on occasion received a signal from as far away as Chicago, or even Mexico.

When I started going to school at the age of 7, we had only a one-room, one-teacher schoolhouse, and I had to walk several miles each day to get there. That was the time of the Great Depression; and although there were bad times, we had plenty of resources to carry us through, since we had on our farm our own garden and our own chickens and cows.

Although I grew up in a simple world on the farm, I am also grateful to have become a part of our modern world of technology. The Lord has given me many interesting experiences as I have traveled around the world. I am privileged to have been to India, there participating one time in a Christian crusade, to the Far East to Japan, and to the Middle East to Egypt, where there were such sights as the Sphinx and the Great Pyramid. My travels have also taken me to Hawaii, and I have flown across both the Pacific and Atlantic Oceans.

My experiences have ranged from the time when riding in a horse-drawn buggy with my mother and grandmother, to my time as a chaplain with the USAF, to more recently being for the last 40 years the pastor of a local church. Ever since 1940, when the Lord called me into special service, I have been a preacher of the Gospel of Christ. Along with preaching the Gospel, there has come a love for the people in my ministry and an attempt to encourage them along the way. Both Wilton's Wit and Wilton's Wit For Children have been an extension of that ministry. My hope is that these essays, taken from the lessons learned in a lifetime of service, are enjoyable to read and that they give the encouragement intended.

I would like to thank all my friends and associates who have encouraged me to write this version of my book. I would like also to give special thanks to my son, Aaron Wilton, who has spent many hours rewriting and preparing the materials for this edition of Wilton's Wit For Children.

Clyde C. Wilton

Wilton's Wit For Children
Table of Contents
(1)

(2)

The Horseless Carriage

Grandpa Wilton did not have a lot of education, but he was a smart man, and he had many interesting things to tell us. Also, he never used bad speech or curse words, and he always had kind things to say. He was called "Uncle Henry" by his friends.

I remember that one of grandpa's favorite stories was about the time he first saw what was called a horseless carriage. It was actually one of the first cars made, and it was strange to the people like Grandpa who lived way out in the country, because all they had to get around in was a buggy or wagon

that was pulled by a horse or a mule. Since cars ran on gasoline, they didn't need anything to pull them along the way. That is why they were called horseless carriages.

Grandpa's house was about 4 miles from a small town called Jermyn, Texas. There was a dirt road that came from Jermyn, Texas, and passed by his house. It continued on down the road to Jacksboro, Texas, which was about twelve miles away.

There were not many people that came along Grandpa's road, and the only real connection with places farther away was by the weekly newspaper. In the newspaper, Grandpa read a little bit about the new horseless carriage, and he hoped that someday he would actually be able to see one.

Well, that happened one day when one of those horseless cars came right up the road and stopped in front of his house!

When this happened, there was

steam coming up out of the front of the car, and the man with the car asked Grandpa if he could have some water to put in his car. Since this was all new to Grandpa, and since he saw the steam coming out of the front, he thought the car must run on steam that came from the water that was put in the car. He didn't realize that the car actually ran on gasoline and was just overheated, causing steam to come out.

Since there was a lot of steam coming out and it looked like they would need a lot of water and quickly, Grandpa thought the best place to go would be to the creek that ran through his property. It had plenty of water and was easy to reach. So, Grandpa got a bucket to hold the water, and he rode in the car with the man down to the creek.

When they got to the creek, the man used only one bucketful of water to fill his car, and that seemed strange to Grandpa, because he had seen so much steam coming from the car. When the man thanked him for the water, Grandpa said, "That won't make enough steam for anything!"

To his surprise, the man said, "This car does not run on steam. It runs on gasoline."

Grandpa's answer was, "Well, Shucks! If I had known that, we could have gotten that much water from the well in my yard!" So, after they had gone to all the trouble of going down to the creek, all they really had to do was go to Grandpa's well nearby. But Grandpa was still happy, because he got his ride in a car for the first time.

Billy And Nanny

One of the best trips I ever took was with my Dad when I was about 6 or 7 years old. I have made many other trips to a lot of different places, but that trip with my Dad was very special.

For the trip that day, we went in our big-wheeled farm

wagon, which had a wooden seat in the front. The wagon was

pulled by two of our horses. The most important thing about the trip was that it was made just for me. Before we left, I knew that Pa was going to get me a present, but I did not know what the big surprise would be.

Our trip took several hours, but the time passed quickly. I can still remember the trip as we left our farmhouse to the Winn Hill Community in Texas. We

passed by several places that I knew about, but then we went to places I had never been before. Finally, we came to a big ranch — at least it was big to me!

Then I got the big surprise that I was waiting for. Pa had bought two little goats just for me! What a thrill that was! It's a thrill even now just thinking about it!

We then returned on the road home. As we brought the goats home in the wagon, I was the happiest boy in our whole area—maybe even the happiest boy in Jack County, Texas!

The two goats, which were all mine to run and jump and play with, were named Billy and Nanny. They became some of my best friends. Later, there were more goats, and Pa fenced off part of our farm just for the

goats. Billy and Nanny were

always special to me, and they were still with us even when I left home to go to college.

Yes, that was a trip to remember! Since that time, I have taken trips by buggy, car, ship, train, and airplane, but never have I been on a trip that made me more happy than that trip in the wagon on that country dirt road to the goat farm. Pa always did the right things. He

had time to be with me and to treat me as somebody important. He lived in a way that was respected and honored by others. I always thought he was the greatest person I ever knew. That is why I have always wanted to be that kind of a Pa.

Aesop's Dog

There was once a great storyteller named Aesop who lived a long time ago in the country of Greece. Although he  was a Greek slave and he did not have a fancy title, he was a great teacher. His students were usually children, and he used animals such as frogs, mice, grasshoppers, birds, wolves, and dogs in his stories.

One of my favorite stories by Aesop is called "The Dog and His Shadow?" In this story,

Aesop tells about a dog that was crossing a smooth, clear stream walking on a wood plank that was laid across the stream. The dog had a large piece of meat in his mouth. As he was passing

over the stream, he looked down into the water and he saw what he thought was another dog, but it was really his own reflection. It looked like there was another dog carrying a piece of meat. He snapped greedily at his shadow, thinking that he might get the other dog's piece of meat, too. But, when he opened his mouth, his own piece of meat fell out of his mouth down, down, far into the stream, and he never saw it again.

That story about the dog is a lot like people today. They are sometimes not satisfied with what they have, and they snap at other people and try to get what they have. The lesson from Aesop is that whenever we are tempted to be greedy, we should remember what happened to Aesop's dog. That should help us to respect other people and be happy with what we have rather than try to take from others.

A Red-Letter Day

A "red-letter day" is one of those days in our lives that are really special to us. It is a day that we remember for many years to come, because it is such a happy day. At one time, people would put a big red letter on that day of the calendar to

remind them that it was so special. That is why it was called a "red-letter" day.

I had one of those red-letter days when I was about five or six years old. The thought of that day still makes me happy. It was when my Pa spent some special time with me.

At that time, our family lived in the country on a small farm in a place called Jack County, Texas. We didn't have much

money, but we raised our food and most of the things we needed from our land. We also grew wheat on the land, and after it was cut down each year, we would make some of it into wheat flour, which would be used to bake bread and other things. But since we did not have machines to make the wheat into flour on our farm, we had to take the wheat to a place called Perrin, Texas.

So one day after we had cut down our wheat, Pa let me go with him to get the wheat made into flour. We went in our big wagon that held a lot of wheat. It was a long trip in the wagon, because where we were going was about 30 miles away. We had to leave before the sun came up, and we did not get back home until after it was dark.

I was excited about making  that long trip with Pa. Ma packed us a lunch, and we were ready to go early in the morning. I was happy that it was just Pa and I on our trip.

It was a great day, but there was one bad thing that happened on our trip. We had two pet squirrels that we had gotten when they were babies. We fed them with a nipple put on a milk bottle when they were small. After they grew up, they were like members of our family. I liked to play with them, so I brought them along with us. But I didn't tell Pa, because I was afraid he would not let me take them with us. I put them in Pa's pockets without telling him about it. I thought that after we were on our trip I would tell him about the squirrels and then it would be OK with him.

But it didn't happen like I wanted it to. A bad thing happened to one of our squirrels. Pa didn't know they were hidden away in his pockets, and when he sat down, he sat on one of them and killed him! That was pretty sad, but I still had one squirrel to play with.

On our trip it seemed like we would never get there, but

finally we did. At Perrin, the place to make our wheat into flour, there were also many other wagons to have their wheat turned into flour. We had another long wait to take our turn with the wheat, but we  finally got our flour made. We then got ready for our trip back home. We had to go another 30 miles in our slow wagon to get back home.

After another long ride, we finally got back home. By that time the sun had gone down and it was getting dark. It was a good trip, because we now had flour to make some good biscuits to go along with the gravy made from our milk cows. Pa and I made the trip in good shape, and we still had one of our squirrels.

The trip was long, but it was special time that I got to spend with Pa, because we had the whole day to ourselves. What a day to remember! Yes, that day was a Red-Letter day, and it still makes me feel happy when I think about it.

Pa's Razor Strap

Pa (that was the name I had for my Dad) used to shave his beard each Sunday morning before we went to church. We lived in a three-roomed house with a front and back porch, and in the bedroom of the house Pa kept a big trunk where he stored his personal things. That is where he kept his razor, his razor strap, and a mug with a brush and soap in it. The razor strap, which was used to sharpen his razor, was made of leather and it was about one and one-half feet long. When he went to shave, there would be a big "thud" after he first lifted the lid and let it fall back on the trunk. He would then scrape the

razor across the razor strap to sharpen it and put water in the mug to soften up the soap for shaving. He would then go out to the front porch to shave.

Pa was not a real teacher, because he did not have a college education—he never even finished high school. So, he didn't have any school learning about how to raise children. But I will always remember one lesson he taught me one Sunday morning when the family went to our church at Winn Hill, which was just a couple of miles from home.

As usual, we rode to church in our Model T car. But on this morning, once we got to church things turned out differently. For some reason, I decided to have some fun with my mother this day. Instead of sitting quietly like I was supposed to, I would slide down one church seat to the middle and then cross over to the other side and slide down to the end of the row. I was having too much fun to listen to the preacher. My mother followed along after me trying to make me behave, but that didn't stop me. While it lasted, it was a fun time.

After church, we got into our car and Pa drove us home. Everything was very quiet as we headed down the road, but I sensed somehow that something was wrong. Pa just wasn't acting the way I thought that he should. So, when the car stopped in front of our house, I made a dash for the side of our house where there was a gap in the stones that lined  the foundation. The wood floor of our house was sitting on a layer of stones, and since some of the stones were missing, I was able to crawl under the house. I thought I would be able to stay out of trouble if I could find a good place to hide under the house.

However, when Pa got out of the car, he went straight for the big trunk in the bedroom. About the time he reached his trunk, I was under the floor of that same room, and when I heard the "thud" of the lid on his trunk, I

knew that bad things were on the way.

Pa was a man of few words, and the only words that I remember him saying that day when he looked under the floor for me were, "Clyde, come out from under there." His voice was not loud, but it was commanding, and I knew that my time of punishment had arrived. I crawled out like a person facing a firing squad, and I met Pa with his razor strap in his hand. He had already shaved, so I knew that he did not need it for his razor. He used it that day for another purpose. It was applied forcefully to my rear end.

After that, I did not give my parents any trouble the next Sunday, or the next, or the next—in fact, that was a lesson that made a lasting impression on me. So, Pa did turn out to be a great teacher, after all, without the need of any fancy book learning, since he certainly taught me a valuable lesson that day. His lesson was that punishment may come after bad behavior.

Miss Edna

Even though we may grow old, the memories of our school days are such happy times for most of us that we may never forget them. That is how I remember my first year of school at the Winn Hill School near my

home in Jack County, Texas. I remember that in our little community of Winn Hill, there was the Bethany Baptist Church, and a short distance up the road across a creek, there was a cemetery and an outside meeting place called a tabernacle. Across the road from the cemetery was the schoolhouse.

The school at Winn Hill had two rooms that were divided by a wall between them, but only

one of the rooms was being used at the time I was there; and, the school had only one teacher. In the schoolroom we used there was a long blackboard, and there was a big potbelly stove that burned wood for heat in the wintertime. At the entrance to the school, there was a cloakroom to hang our coats and a place to put our sack lunches. At Winn Hill the first grade was called a Primer class, and classes continued up through the  seventh grade. After finishing the school grades provided at Winn Hill, students then went to Jermyn High School, which was several miles away in the town of Jermyn, Texas.

The one thing that impressed me the most about the Winn Hill School was the teacher. Her name was Edna Meyers, but we called her, "Miss Edna." We were taught the usual subjects, but I remember that one of the hardest things for me to learn was the multiplication table.

For our reading lessons, we used one of the best books I have ever read. Its title was "Baby Ray." One of the things I remember about the book was the story about a boy named Baby Ray, who had a dog. He loved his dog so much that his dog loved him back! He also had other animals, and he loved all of them, and they loved him. What made the time so special was that our teacher, Miss Edna, also had that same kind of love for us. She loved us, and that is why we loved her so much.

That time was about 1926, and I have had many teachers over the years, but none were more important to me than my first teacher, Miss Edna.

When Miss Edna came to our school, she had just finished college, and Winn Hill was her first school to teach. Even though she did not have much experience, she taught us with such loving concern that she still brings happy memories. She reminds me of a mother hen with her wings spread out to cover all her chicks.

Often, at the close of the school day, a young man by the name of Fred Shields would be waiting to take Miss Edna home. Later, they were married and her last name was changed to "Shields." As time passed by, she had children of her own and she became a grandmother, and later her husband died. But through all of this, she was then and is to this day still "Miss Edna" to me.

Another lasting thing that I remember about this special teacher was that she gave to all of her students a little Bible New Testament. I had mine for many years, and I still carry it around in my mind and my heart. Things are so different today, because now the public schools do not allow teachers to give out Bibles. It is my opinion that even though a lot of things have gotten better in school since I left, keeping Bibles out of school did not make them better. I Thank God for teachers like "Miss Edna," because her love has had such a lasting effect on others!

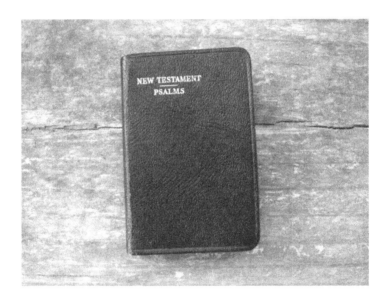

The Buggy Ride

When I was a young boy of about 5 or 6 years of age, I had one of the most exciting rides of my life. On that day, I was with Ma (my mother), and Grandma Wilton, and we planned to visit my Aunt Amy Parrish, Uncle Jake, and my cousins, Hazel and Herbert (I called him Herb). It

was such a special treat for me, because I loved to play with my cousin Herb. They lived about 4 miles from where we lived.

To get to the Parrish place, we would first go over a steep hill called the Easter Hill, which

was just down the road from our house, and then we would pass through a valley and a winding road before we got to their house. It brought happy feelings to me as I thought about the trip we were going to take and the day I was planning to spend with Herb.

Our way to travel then was in a buggy that was pulled by a horse or a mule. For this trip we went in Grandma's buggy, and it

was pulled by our mule, who had the name of "Old Ider." So, after hitching Old Ider to the buggy, we were off on the trip.

As we traveled about a half-mile down the road from our house, we came to the Easter Hill. The hill was very steep and the road turned to the right at the bottom of the hill. The one

driving the buggy that day was Grandma Wilton. She was a good driver, but while she was holding the reins in her hand, which was the leather strap that controlled the mule, an awful thing happened as we started over the hill. Somehow, Old Ider got her tail caught in the reins and that cut off all control that Grandma had for driving the buggy. When Grandma lost control, Old Ider took off down the steep Easter Hill on her own, and what a ride that turned out to be!

At the bottom of the hill there were some big ditches that were deep and wide. After a short but exciting ride down Easter Hill, our buggy turned over and landed upside down in one of the big ditches. The buggy was then on top of us, and we were in the ditch. Old Ider got loose from the buggy and ran down the road, and she finally stopped in the Easter family's cotton patch.

After climbing out of the ditch, Ma, Grandma, and I started walking back up the Easter Hill and back home. Later, some of our family and friends caught Old Ider and brought her home. They also brought back the broken pieces of the buggy that belonged to Grandma and Grandpa.

The day began with a happy feeling, but it didn't end that way. However, there were no bones broken or serious injury, so we were still thankful for that.

We never got to the Parrish farm that day, but we got a ride that we will never be forgotten. As far as I can remember, that was my last buggy ride. It really had a good ending, even though the buggy was broken into many pieces. I still thank God for my last buggy ride.

Help

Have you ever needed help badly? Not too long ago I had to call 911 for emergency help, because my wife was in serious need of care. As was the case with my wife, many of us would be in serious trouble sometimes if there were not other people who were willing to help.

I am reminded of the Bible story by the name of the "Good Samaritan." It was about a man from a place called Samaria. That is why he was called a Samaritan, because he was from Samaria, and he did a good deed for a man one day who was in need of help. While this man from Samaria was traveling in a place called Judea, he found a man on the side of the road who had been robbed and was dying.

It was strange, because before this good man came by, two other religious people, who were supposed to care for people in need, had just passed on by the dying man, because they had more important religious jobs to take care of. In Judea, where the dying man was robbed, the people there did not like Samaritans. But in spite of the fact that the Samaritan was in the wrong place because of where his home was, he stopped to see what he could do for the man in need, because he had love for the man in his heart. It was with the help of the Samaritan man that the dying man recovered.

One time I was also in need of help. It was in the year 1959. At that time, I had just started a new Air Force job in the country of Japan. I had left my family in Texas to move to the other side of the world to Japan. I was also allowed to bring a car with me, but it came in a big ship after I had left Texas.

When the ship that carried all the cars came, they were kept at a city about 20 miles away. A group of us had to go by bus to that city to get our cars.

The bus that carried us to the city for our cars did not stay long, and it left us behind after we left the bus to go to our cars.

The other people I was with that day did not have any trouble with their cars, and when they got in their cars, they drove up a nearby hill and out of sight. However, even though my car started when I first got in, it then quit and would not start again.

When my car would not go, I was left in that strange city with no friends. The sun was just barely up and it was about to go down, so it would soon be dark. I could see some Japanese people out in the distance, but it was a strange place for me and I didn't speak their language.

Everyone had left me, and I had no idea of how to get back to my new home in Japan. I was a very long distance from my old home in Texas. I was beginning to get scared! But, just before the sun went down, I heard a helicopter coming near where I was, and it landed nearby. An Air Force pilot got out of the helicopter and went to his car that was also near my car. He

had come to pick up his car, but he also helped me with mine. He is what I would call my "Good Samaritan," because he also rescued me when I needed help.

These stories tell me that we should also help others when they need help. We should never be too busy to be a "Good Samaritan" to someone else if they need our help.

Grandpa's Advice

When I was a boy, I used to go visit with Grandpa and Grandma Wilton, who lived about a half mile from our house, and they always had good advice to give me. In the wintertime, we would hover around the wood stove in their living room to keep warm.

One time while visiting with Grandpa, he told me about an experience that was very meaningful for him. It all happened at the time of harvest one year. At that time, there was a church meeting in the community with a special preacher who was giving the message of the gospel of eternal life. At one point, Grandpa and his neighbor met to talk awhile at the fence line of their farms.

The neighbor told Grandpa about the wonderful gospel meeting he was expecting to go to, and he invited Grandpa to come and join him. Since it was harvest time and the cotton needed to be picked, Grandpa told him that he just did not have time to go to the meeting.

When the neighbor heard this excuse, he said to Grandpa, "If you could get to heaven, along with all your family, wouldn't that be more important than all the cotton in the world?" After Grandpa thought about it a minute, he decided that his neighbor was right. So, Grandpa and his family went to the meeting. It turned out to be a great meeting for many who went, and Grandpa was always grateful for the advice that he received that day.

As we were hovering around the wood-burning stove that day listening to Grandpa, I also took the advice about the gospel that good man had given to Grandpa. I went home that day richer in my mind than when I came. Whenever I think about it, in my mind I still gather around that stove as I did when I was a young boy on that winter day listening to that beautiful story. If we are willing, we can benefit

from a lot of advice from good
people all around us even today.

Thank You

We have many reasons to say, "Thank You," and mean it. Our lives are a part of so many others that it is hard to imagine doing well without them.

To show how important it is to appreciate others when they help, I like the story told by a teacher at the school where I learned to become a preacher. He tells about a great organ player who gave one of his

concerts. At that time the organs were built in a way that someone had to pump air in behind the organ to make them work.

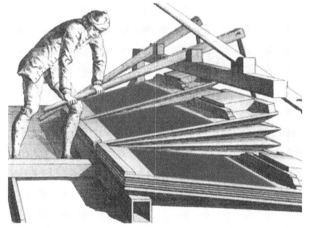

At the end of the first half of the concert by this great organ player, the people clapped loudly showing how much they enjoyed the music. The organist said to one of his friends, "I seemed to have done a good job."

At the beginning of the second half of the concert, with pride the organ player seated himself and began to play again, but this time when he pressed down on the organ keys expecting more lovely music to come out, there was nothing but silence. He quickly made some adjustments on the organ and then pressed down on the keys again, but there was still no music. After a painful delay and  looking around to find why there was no sound, he found the helper who was supposed to pump air into the organ off to the side laughing to himself. The organ player angrily came at the helper, but the helper said, "You bragged a while ago that you did such a good job that I just wanted you to know that you should have given credit to others who make the music possible. You can't get music out of the front end without some way to pump air into the back end."

Our lives are a lot like that, because there are a lot of things that we can't do very well without the help of others. There are a lot of people that we need to say thank-you to, such as our parents, our teachers, our doctors, our ministers, and others who help us in many ways. So, we should never forget the magic words, "Thank You."

The Need For Friends

One of our great needs in the world is to have friends. We need to have friends so we can share our lives with them, because without friends, life would be dull and not very interesting.

My first friendship was from my parents when I was a baby.  That was when I received tender loving care from them that I have been thankful for throughout my life.

I vividly remember my early days on our small farm in North

Texas. My parents were poor as far as having nice things, but I never doubted they were rich in love for me. We would go to Jacksboro (a city of about 4,000 people) about two times a month to buy some of our groceries. I fondly remember that Pa would buy me a nickel's worth of candy in a small

paper sack, and sometimes he would get me a big piece of chewing gum.

Much later, when it was time for me to go off to college, I remember that I left my mother in tears, because she did not want to see her baby boy leave home.

My time in college was new to me, and for the first time I had to provide for myself. There were some big changes, and I met some new friends. In my new experience, I thought I could handle just about anything that came my way. However, I quickly found some things that I hadn't planned for. The first time I tried to iron my white shirt, I burned a hole in the sleeve. I then decided that it would be cheaper for me to send my shirts to the laundry.

When it came my turn to do some cooking for the other college students where we lived, I thought I would cook a plateful of beans. So, I got the big dishpan and filled it full of pinto beans and turned up the heat. Sometime later, the smell of burned beans filled the house. For the first time, I was beginning to appreciate what my parents had done for me over the years. In my mind, the smell of those burned beans still lingers in my nose!

For a while, it was a thrill to be away from home and to live with other young men of my age. But I also remember my longing to go back home and be with my parents and other friends once more.

Finally the day came. Pa met me in Jacksboro one Saturday afternoon. When I had been a kid, my concern was about what he could give me, such as candy and chewing gum. But now, the thrill was not what he could give me, but the thrill was just to be in his presence again and to talk to him and enjoy his friendship.

There is another kind of friendship that is even more important. That is the friendship we can have with our heavenly Father. When we are new, baby Christians, we are often more concerned about what he can do for us. We ask for many things, and he provides our needs. But when we are more mature Christians, we become more concerned just about his daily presence. We come to realize that the most awesome of all experiences in the entire world is to have sweet fellowship with the Almighty God. He is the Friend of all friends, and his friendship gives real meaning to life.

The Windmill

I was taught a big lesson one day by someone who first thought he knew a lot about someone but really did not. A church member named Jack asked me to help him repair a windmill near our church. So, both of us climbed on the tower under the big wheel of the windmill to fix it. As we  began our work, Jack started to tell me about one of his neighbors, but before he said anything he stopped himself and said, "I don't know enough about that man to talk about him." Then he changed what he was going to say and never said another word about his neighbor.

That day with Jack made me think a lot about the world we live in. There are so many things to know, but there is just not enough time in all the time we live here to learn them. This even happens with people who have important jobs, like doctors and scientists. They don't really know so much. And when we look at other people, we think we know a lot about them by how they look and how they act, but we really don't.

That was a great lesson for me, and since that time I have heard in my mind many times the words Jack said, "I don't know enough about that man to talk about him." I am thankful to Jack for the lesson that he taught me that day that since we know so little about so many things, we  should be careful about what we say about other people.

Thoughts

Did you know that what you think is really who you are? What you do  and what you say may not be exactly who you are, but what you think is the real you.

Also, you may not be what others say you are. You are probably better than what some people think you are, and you may be worse than what others think you are.

There are other things about you that may not be the real you.

You may not be what your clothes say about you. Some people dressed in ragged clothes may want to help others, but those who are dressed in the finest clothes may even be bad people looking for a way to take advantage of others.

You are not what you eat. You are more than the meat and vegetables that help to build your body.

But, again, you are your thoughts, because your thoughts are actually you. Since you are your thoughts, one of the greatest needs is to think good thoughts. A famous writer once said, "The happiest man is he who thinks the most interesting thoughts," and I think he was right.

If you are thinking thoughts of fear and worry, you are not thinking good thoughts. Those thoughts just make you feel bad. But even if things around you seem bad, if you think good thoughts anyway, you can still be happy.

In the Bible there is the story about the preacher named Paul. Even though at one time he was tied to a heavy chain and guarded by a soldier, he was glad and happy, because he had spent at lot of time praying and thinking about good things rather than trying to get even with those who treated him badly. Paul was more interested in what God thought about him than what other people thought.

I think we can actually say that good thoughts are worth more than good clothes, or fine food, or anything else, because good thoughts are more a lasting part of us.

If you think about it, what we did and thought about yesterday is the cause of what we are thinking about today; and what we will be doing tomorrow is a result of our thoughts today. So, it is always a good thing to think good thoughts.

So, you should always remember that the most important thing about you is your thoughts, because the real you is what you think.

The Bible way of telling us about good thoughts says it even better. The Bible says it this way: "Whatsoever a man thinks in his heart, so is he."

LaRue Vivian Haley

It was a great day for me when I left home and went to college, even though I left my mother in tears. I first went to college at Weatherford, Texas, and quickly made new friends. However, since my cousin and

lifelong friend, Herbert Parrish, was a student at Denton, Texas, I transferred to Denton to be near him.

While I was there, a very strange thing happened to me.  After the Lord got my attention by making me wonder about where we are going after this life on earth, I accepted his invitation to be a minister of the gospel of Jesus Christ. I then left college and went back to the farm to live with my parents for more than a year.

In 1941, I again entered college, but this time I went to a

Christian school by the name of Howard Payne College, which is located in Brownwood, Texas. It was there that I met LaRue Vivian Haley, who became my

wonderful wife for almost 61 years. We came to college from different ends of the state, and we both were working to earn enough to stay in college.

I started at Howard Payne College before LaRue did, and on October 17, 1943, after I graduated, we got married. Over the years between 1945 and 1958, we had four children.

LaRue was a very devout Christian. Starting in 1952, I joined the United States Air Force as a chaplain, and we were forced to move many times because of my job. LaRue was always willing to go wherever my job took us, whether it was to Hawaii, Japan, or other places.

LaRue's mother was also a very wonderful person. Granny Haley, which is what we called her, lived in a small house in a place called Hargill, Texas. At one point in 1955, when we returned to Texas from Hawaii, I was working at a place called Harlingen, Texas, which was just about 37 miles from Hargill. A couple years later, my job took me to Mission, Texas, which was 37 miles on the other side of

Hargill. It was amazing to me that these two places where I worked were the only bases in the world that were near Granny Haley, and they were at the same distance from her home. I will always believe

that the orders for those jobs were directed by God, who is so much bigger than the United States Air Force.

LaRue loved the Bible and studied it daily, and she lived by what it says. LaRue was also a precious mother, a lovely wife,

and a loyal friend to her relatives and many others. She was also good at keeping the records of our time and money.

Unfortunately, for the last 23 years of her life, LaRue had a disease called Parkinson's. We went to many doctors, but they could not do anything to cure her disease, and she gradually got weaker.

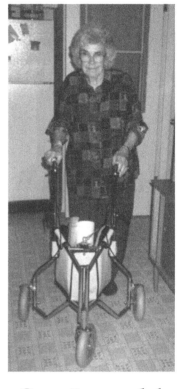

For the last 119 days of her life, LaRue remained very sick. After first being at the St. Joseph's Health Center in Bryan, she was later admitted to a hospital in San Antonio. While she was in San Antonio, LaRue told me that she wanted to spend her last days at our home in Bryan. So, to follow what she wanted, her last 5 days were spent in her own bed at home.

While she was sick, LaRue could only say what she wanted by writing on a paper tablet, and at times it was very difficult to

understand her messages. One day, LaRue wrote the note, "Wouldn't it be wonderful if I could wake up someday without

Parkinson's Disease?" I agreed that it would, and I believe that where she is now in heaven she is free from all disease.

For almost 61 years, I told LaRue that I loved her before we went to sleep at night. I never tired of telling her so, and she never seemed to tire of me telling her of my deep feelings for her. She was truly my "better half."

Good Food

Do you ever feel empty and hungry? Usually, that feeling does not last for very long if we eat our regular meals every day. It would be foolish for a person to try to eat food to live on for months at a time — in fact, the person who would not accept food daily would be considered rather strange and in need of medical help.

It would be just as strange if people decided to go looking for their food in  garbage cans. Usually, that only happens when poor people cannot find food any other way. It would be really strange for someone to prefer what they found in garbage cans to a regular meal set out on the dinner table.

Did you know that we also have daily needs that are not provided by bread or regular food. What I am saying is that God has placed a daily need to communicate with him and to follow the things he wants us to do, which is supplied by what we call spiritual food. Just as it is strange and unhealthy to try to cram food into our bodies to last for a longer time or to look in the garbage can for our physical food, there are times that we try to do that with our daily spiritual food.

For example, rather than praying daily and going to church each week, some people only do these things rarely or just a couple of times each year, thinking that is enough to fill their spiritual needs. But just as there is a daily need for bread, there is also a daily need for spiritual food.

Also, some people spend so much of their time watching television and playing video games and doing other things that they don't have much time to feed their spirit. That is just like looking for food in the wrong places.

I believe that regular spiritual food is just as important as daily bread. It is God's desire for us to receive regular spiritual food, because it is His desire for us to enjoy all good things. That is the way we can have a life that is good and healthy!

Love

I believe that the greatest of all things in the world is love. Love is what makes us happy and able to enjoy being with others. Our homes would fall apart without love, and the parents might even leave the children behind unwanted and unloved, without it. Without love, our country would be in trouble, because no one would be interested in living by the laws. Without love, the world would not have peace, because there would be no reason to respect other countries.

The members of one of the early Christian churches had many wonderful gifts. With the help from God, they were wise in many things and they could do things like heal and do mighty miracles. But they were lacking in one important thing. They did not love one another as they should.

These Christians were informed by the Apostle Paul

that the gift of love was worth more than all their other gifts put together. In fact, he said that this gift of love was so far ahead of the other gifts that they were actually worthless without this gift of love.

So, to love God and to love others ought to be one of the most important things for everyone to seek, because the Bible tells us that God is love!

Silent Affect

There are two kinds of ways that affect other people. One way is to talk right at someone to try to get him to understand or to do something. That is usually done by teaching, or arguing, or threatening, or by giving a gift, or even by making a promise. Then, there is the silent effect we may have on someone, without saying anything to them. This comes from just the kind of person we are, and we can affect others without really being aware of it.

Some people say that this silent effect is actually more important than what we say. Even if someone does good at a job such as being a teacher, or a plumber, or a salesman, or a senator, or a lawyer, or a doctor, or even as a president, if they don't have a good silent effect, they may not have a good effect on others.

For example, if a leader gives great speeches and makes us promises, but we know by his silent effect and from his past actions that he will not really do what he says, then we won't take him seriously or follow him. However, if we know from his silent effect that he is honest and he really cares about what he says, we are more likely to support and follow what he wants us to do. So, a person's silent effect actually speaks louder to us than what he says with his words.

I have learned that when people live by the Golden Rule, which tells us "to do to others how you want them to treat you," we can have that good

silent effect. In the Bible, Jesus has said that He is as much interested by our silent effect, or the way we are inside, and that we have respect for others, as he is by what we say to others.

The Honey Bee

The honeybee is a very important insect. When we think of honeybees we usually think about the honey they make, and that is a good food source for us, but did you know that they are even more valuable because they also gather pollen from plants for their food? Some  of the pollen that they carry as they go from one flower to another gets left behind on the flowers. It is the pollen left on the flowers that helps the plants grow into healthy new plants.

There are hundreds of different kinds of bees in the world, but most of them do not live together but live alone. The honeybee is different from those other kinds of bees, because it lives in a big group, called a beehive. In their group, they

have three different jobs. There is the Queen Bee, who lays the bee eggs, and they have only one of those. Then there are worker bees, who are female bees, and drone bees, who are the male bees. The first of the honeybees that came to America came about the year 1638 when they were brought by the early people who came to America.

I was first introduced to the honeybee when I was a young lad. My Pa liked to hunt the  bees and eat their honey, and he brought beehives home and put them in our peach orchard. One summer, I remember that he had about 13 beehives in our orchard.

One time, Pa bought a queen bee from Sears, Roebuck & Company, and in the wintertime he put her and her beehive in the roof of the barn, along with hay surrounding the hive. The bees did not survive the winter. Pa did not realize at the time that it took time for a new beehive to fix its hive for living through the winter, and Pa started that beehive too late in the year for it to survive. Of course, we were disappointed that the beehive failed, but the experience with the bees made me interested in keeping bees for many years after that.

There are many things about honeybees that are interesting, but one thing that amazes me is how the  honeybee can pass information to the other bees in the beehive. It is the worker bees that leave the beehive to search for flowers that are making nectar, which the bees make into honey. When they find nectar, they bring it back to the beehive, and with a movement called a "wagtail dance," they tell the other bees exactly where the flowers are so they can also get the nectar.

Where I live, in Bryan, Texas, I live only a few miles from the "bee capitol of the world." That is the name given to the bee business of the Weaver family living at Lynn Grove, Texas. They sell thousands of queen bees each year throughout the world.

Lost Without Knowing It

Have you ever been lost but did not know it? I was one time. It turned out OK, though, because I was found, even before I really knew that I was lost.

This happened to me when I was a boy. In those days people sometimes had church outside in what was called a tabernacle.

This was an outside building made from wood posts in the

ground that held up a roof and was open on all sides to the air. Under the roof there would be benches to sit on that were placed on the dirt ground. Churches would go in together and have a preacher come for a week or two to preach. When this happened, a lot of people from the area would come to the tabernacle.

The meeting where I went to that day was at a place called Jermyn, Texas. It was about four miles away from our farm. So, our whole family—my Pa, my Ma, my two brothers, and I— went to the meeting.

This kind of meeting usually took a long time, so it was allowed for people to come in and go out during the meeting if they needed to. During the meeting, my brothers went outside, so I followed them. They began talking with our neighbor, named Obert McCarty,

who came to the meeting in his Model T car. While they were talking, I climbed up into the back seat of Obert's car, which was just a few feet away, and I went to sleep.

I do not remember anything else about the church service that day, and when Obert left the meeting, I was still asleep in the back of Obert's Model T car. He lived about five and a half miles away. That was why I said I was lost but did not know it, because I was still asleep in his car and didn't know he had left the meeting and my family behind.

When the meeting at the tabernacle was over, everyone thought I was lost, because I couldn't be found. People were sent out in every direction to look for me. Pa and Ma were upset, but no one could find me.

When Obert got to his home, he drove his car into his dark garage. He had put some mail in the back seat earlier, so when he reached in the back seat to get his mail, there he found me fast asleep. That was quite a surprise for Obert, but when he found me, he took me back to the tabernacle. Then my folks had a

sigh of relief, and the story had a happy ending. So I had been lost but didn't know it, and I was found before I even knew I was lost.

The Moment Of Truth

I grew up on a farm in Jack County, Texas, which was about 50 miles away from the big city of Fort Worth. In my family, besides myself, there were my parents and my two older brothers. By the way they taught us and the way they acted, my parents were a good Christian example for me and my brothers to follow.

However, by the time I was a teenager, I thought I was so grown up that I began to question the teachings of my parents. I began to think that my mother was old-fashioned and outdated and that my dad seemed too interested in making sure we all had enough work to do. Ever since we lived on our own small farm,  we had always depended on the family to get things done around the farm, and there seemed to always be something that needed to be done. But there came a time when I was a teenager that I began to wonder if I wanted that farm life any longer.

Then, when I was old enough to go to college, I jumped at the chance to leave home and be on my own away from the farm. For the first few

 months after I went to school at the Weatherford Jr. College, I had a great time. I could do anything I

wanted to and I thought I knew about everything that I needed to know about life. Since there was no one there to tell me otherwise, I began trying out some things that were new to me. I tried drinking a little bit of beer, did some dancing, and gambled some at playing cards, things I had been taught at home that were not right for a good Christian to be doing. I kept telling myself that these things were not so bad, after all. I was so busy with my new interests that I didn't even have enough time to go to church.

Then something strange happened. God got my attention

by making me think about what would happen after I left this life. That was the idea that we have a life after the one here on earth and that it lasts forever on  into eternity. That was early in the year 1940, and I remember looking on as my fellow students were going in all directions to their classes and other activities. While they were busy attending to their present duties, all I could think about was the idea of, "Where are we going to spend eternity!" I had a miserable two or three weeks trying to make sense out of all these thoughts.

What was really going on was that God had a job for me to do and He was trying to get my attention. When I realized what was happening, I eventually listened to what he was trying to tell me. What he wanted me to

do was to become a preacher. After I agreed to what He wanted, all those strange questions stopped and I was sure that I was finally headed in the right direction.

It was then that I went back to the farm, where I stayed for about another year and a half. I went back to my home church at the Bethany Baptist Church, and in March 1940 I preached my first sermon. The Lord showed me that going to church, praying, and studying the scriptures was far better than a desire to be worldly by dancing, drinking, and playing poker. When I realized how holy God was and how fortunate I was to be useful in his service, I realized that Pa and Ma had really taught me well and that they were not so dumb after all.

The Power Of Prayer

Do you pray to God each day? Do you really know what prayer is for? It is more than just saying the same words each time you try to pray, and it is more than telling God what you need. Did you know that the real reason for praying is to find out what God is doing and to find how we can work into His plans?  When we pray, we should be more concerned about what we need to do to fit into his will than to try to change his plans for our benefit.

An example is with the prophet Elijah in the Bible. There is the story that he prayed for it not to rain, and for three years and six months it did not rain.

Then later he prayed for it to rain and the rain came. Did that mean that, by praying, Elijah had power to control the weather? The answer comes by what Elijah later said, himself. He said, "O Lord, the God of Abraham, Isaac, and Israel, let it be known this day that I am your servant and that I have done all these things at your word." So it was not Elijah's idea at all. He just found out what God wanted him to do and he did it.

So, it is important to remember that God does want us to communicate with him through prayer, but the real power in prayer is learning what he is planning to do and then fitting what we do into his plans.

Salmon In Ketchikan

In 2004, I was able to visit in Ketchikan, Alaska, which has been called the "Salmon Capital of the World." While there, I stayed with the Terry Sivertsen family, who were relatives of my son-in-law, Robert Worley.

While in Alaska, I got to see two eagles, an owl, and a sparrow hawk that were injured.

They could not be put back into their home in the forest, because they would not live since they were so badly hurt. We were told that an eagle can see four times better than a man. An eagle can see tiny things as far away as the length of a football field, and when it is flying high into the air it can see two feet under the water.

Terry Sivertsen and I also visited the place where they raise salmon in Ketchikan. They raise new salmon each year to put back into the ocean. The place where we went raises about 100,000 new salmon each year.

One female King Salmon can make up to 5000 eggs. The eggs are first put into trays to grow, and it then takes two 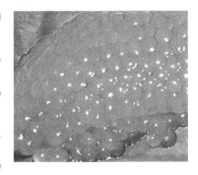 years before the salmon are large enough to let go. The small fish is called a Smolt at the time it leaves.

About three years after the young salmon leave, they return back home to the same place

where they left. They are able to find their home by the smell and taste of the water. The record size for the King Salmon is about 100 pounds.

At Ketchikan they also raise Rainbow Trout, but they are much smaller than salmon. The largest size for the trout is about 40 pounds. The trout tastes very good, but Terry said the King Salmon tastes much better than the trout.

It was a lot of fun to visit Alaska, and there were a lot of other things to see besides the salmon. Someday, if you get the chance, you should also go to see Alaska.

Our Fast Time

We are living in a time when everything seems to move fast. We have fast food, fast cars, fast computers, and fast connections with almost everything. We do not like to wait for anything. We want things to happen now!

Things were different when I was growing up. Yes, I grew up in the country, where things were slower and it was not very important to move fast. The main people in my little world were my Pa and my Ma and my two brothers. Grandpa and Grandma lived about a half mile away; over the hill about a mile lived some friends by the name of the Kinnards and the Hubers; and about a mile in another direction over a hill we called the Easter Hill was Ernest Easter and his family. Back behind us there was nothing but trees and bushes and rocks that went on for miles.

Even though things were slower at our country home, we had most of the things we needed. We had cows that give us milk, and hogs that give us meat, and we had a large garden for vegetables and a hen house with chickens that provided fresh eggs. For our work, we didn't have to travel far, because most of our work was just on the

other side of our cow lot, and our working hours were from when the sun came up until the sun went down. There was plenty to do, so there was no need to be in a hurry.

The biggest city in the area was Jacksboro, Texas, which was about 12 miles away. We went to our "Big City" of Jacksboro only about twice each month to get a few supplies, such as flour, cornmeal, sugar, salt, pepper, soap, and medicine for our

medicine drawer. We also went there sometimes on Saturday

afternoons for fun, because there was a movie house on the second floor of the Spears Drug Store, where it cost about 10 or 15 cents to see the movie. Saturday was also special for me, because I could meet there with my cousin, Herbert Parrish, who would also usually be there. We  enjoyed going up and down the streets, and if we had five cents we could get a hamburger. Those were days that bring happy memories!

Since we were not in a hurry in the country, we were

not really concerned about communicating with the rest of the world. If we needed to, we could write a letter and send it anywhere in the United States for 2 cents, and a post card cost only a penny. We had a

telephone line hooked up to Grandma's house, which was about a half mile away, and I can remember that at one time we were hooked up all the way to Uncle Jakes' house, which was about 3 miles away. Our telephone was a big red box about 2 feet high and about 1 foot wide. We had to put two large batteries about the size of a pickle jar in the telephone box to make it work. Calls were made with a small crank located on the side of the box.

That was the world that I grew up in, so even today, I am not too happy about today's fast living. Rather than going to some fast food place, I am happy to just put some beans in the crockpot in the morning, let them cook all day, and then just enjoy a great bean banquet in the evening! For me, it just "doesn't get any better than that!"

The Best Seller

To be able to read is one of the great joys for people. Our bookstores are filled with all kinds of books and other things to read. There are a lot of good things to read.

One of the best books ever written was the best seller, or the one that sold the most books, last year. In fact, the book I am talking about has been a best seller now for many years. This book is an unusual one. It is about things that have happened during 2,000 years, and about 44 different people have written parts of the book to prepare it for readers. The book I am talking about is the Holy Bible.

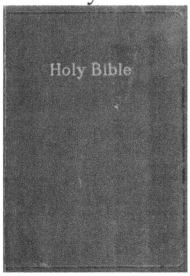

The Bible is actually a lot of books put together to make one book. It is divided into two big parts, which are called, the Old Testament and the New Testament. In the Old Testament we are told about how the world began and about what happened to the first man, who was named Adam, and his family. It is about the people God chose to be his special people.

The New Testament tells about the birth and life of Jesus. It tells about his church and his message to the world. His message, called the good news, has brought happiness to many people.

The Bible is such an important book, that it is written

in almost every language in the world.

A Point of View

If you think about where you are today, you will have to agree that you can only live in the present. Yesterday is gone, and tomorrow hasn't come yet, so all we have is the present. Since we will never be able to live today again, maybe we should take it very seriously as it goes by. Later, we may want to go back to live this day again, but we know that can't happen. The Creator made it so we cannot slow down or speed up the time we have to live in.

I am reminded of the time that I visited the Great Pyramid

of Giza, one of the Seven Wonders of the Ancient World. Nearby was a huge stone statue called the Sphinx, which was carved to look like a lion's body with a human face, and also

nearby was the famous Nile River and the city of Cairo, Egypt. Together with me were a Catholic priest and a guide who was of the Muslim religion. Although we were from different religions, we were together that day for the job of climbing the pyramid to see the world from its top. Although we did not agree about religion, we were there together for a time to do an important job in the present. We could not say how things might be the next day or into the future.

Even though those other people on the pyramid had a different point of view, or saw things differently from me, the

Bible tells me that if we are Christians, we can live in the present and still be prepared for the things of the future ahead. The Bible tells us that Christ can make us strong enough to handle all things that may come our way.

Changing The Price Tags

A famous storyteller once told about a man who broke into a department store one night. But rather than stealing the store's things, he just moved the price tags around on everything. The next day when the store was opened, everyone was surprised to find valuable things like diamonds priced just for a dollar, but the cheap Jewelry was priced for thousands of dollars.

Even though that was just a story, it seems like something

that has happened to us in our country. I am not talking about the price of the things we buy, but I mean the way we treat our ways of doing things. At one time we thought treating others fairly was important, and using

> **To Do
> The Right Thing
> Is Important
> In God's Sight**

bad drugs and too much alcohol should not be done. But now these values do not seem very important to a lot of people. You would think that church people at least would still do the right things, but even many church people seem to act the same as the rest.

It is really sad that people are now less concerned about what can happen when they go against what God has said is bad for us to do. I am reminded about what it says in the Bible in the days of Isaiah, who said, "Ah, you who call evil good and good evil, who put darkness for light and light for darkness, who put bitter for sweet and sweet for bitter!" That sounds a lot like it has become in our time.

When it comes to doing what's right, I think we should put the right price on things. It seems only right to make being good more valuable and being smart, being fair more valuable than just getting what you want, and treating God's ways as more valuable than our own selfish ways.

Communication

If we think about it, we have a lot of ways of communicating, or meeting and talking, with others in our time. We have the telephone, cell phones, e-mail, radio and television, and personal ipods, just to name a few. Most of these modern gadgets were not around when I was born in 1919.

At that time, in the small community of Winn Hill, Texas where I lived, we were not connected very well with the rest of the world. About the time I started school, we got our first telephone, but it was not like modern telephones. It was only connected with a local line that included my grandparents, who lived a half mile away, and my Uncle Jake and Aunt Amy and up to a total of about eight people. On our local line, when  the telephone rang, it used different long and short rings to let people on the line know who the call was for. The telephone also worked using batteries.

When I started to school, I walked with my older brother, Anthony, each day. When we went over the hill near our home and out of sight, there was no way to communicate with our parents until we came back later in the afternoon. For me, I remember that the mile and a half was a long walk. My mother was home all day long by herself. Pa worked on the farm and sometimes with his small herd of cattle. When he

 left the house and was out of sight, except for the time he came home for lunch and a short nap, he was on the job

away from the house.

Back in those days, we never missed today's modern gadgets, because we never even dreamed that they were even possible. However, there were a few people we thought were "nuts" who brought up the strange idea that the time would come when people would be sending pictures through the air. And it was really unbelievable to think that someone might even go to the moon!

However, we did have a mailman that we could depend on. We could send a letter anywhere in the USA for two cents and a postcard for one cent, but their speed was not very fast by today's standards. As an example of how slow things were at times, when my Pa's brother was kicked by a mule and died at a farm just 25 miles away, he was already buried before the family got the message about his brother dying.

But, isn't it great that today we are so hooked up with the world? When something on the other side of the world happens, we hear about it in minutes. In my own house, we have two telephones—one is on my desk, and I have a cell phone. Besides having the telephones we have radios, televisions, and even computers that hook us up with the world. Today we have so much to be thankful for, and there is also the responsibility to use our gadgets for good purposes.

Christmas 2001

I don't know if you know it or not, but there was a time just before the year 2000 that a lot of people thought that when the year 1999 changed to the year 2000 there might be serious problems all over the world.

However, the year 2000 came, and the sun still came up and went down as usual, and the world did not end as some people who claimed to know were telling us. In the year that followed in 2001, we still had the same joy of preparing for the

Christmas season. The false alarm that upset so many people should make us realize that we need to work on God's time schedule rather than some foolish men.

I recall that in my early years, Christmas was the biggest day of the year for us who lived out in the country near a little town called Jermyn, Texas. We prepared for the occasion by getting gifts for our friends and wondering what gifts we might receive from them. Our parents would prepare by getting extra food for the season. This one time of the year we usually had such treats as apples, oranges, walnuts, almonds, and coconuts. Of course, Santa Claus would deliver them on Christmas Eve about midnight. And Santa Claus always came on the eve of the birthday of Jesus. In my Sunday School class we were told about the birth of Jesus, but back then my attention was on Santa  Claus, who seemed like a real friend to me.

However, I later learned that the really important thing about Christmas, or December 25, was that it was supposed to be the birthday of Jesus. That was why we honored Jesus on that day by celebrating giving gifts to one another.

Then, one year I learned that someone claimed that the 25th of December was not really the birthday of Jesus, because he was not even born in December.

For a while, that used to bother me, but really it doesn't bother me anymore. I am convinced that Jesus was not born in December, but that fact is not really important. But the fact that Jesus came and later gave his life for us does make the difference.

So, I am not certain about the exact day of the birth of Jesus, but one thing I am certain about is that 25 December was the birthday of my grandpa, Henry

Franklin Wilton. So, when we met on Christmas Day, it was an extra special day, because we remembered both Jesus and my Grandpa.

So, as we think about the Christmas time again, regardless of when the actual day of his birth was, we should be thrilled with the idea of Jesus being born in Bethlehem, with the story of the Shepherds, and the Wise Men coming to worship him. The gift of salvation that he offers is so much more than Santa Claus could ever give.

I hope that it will be a very happy time for you this next Christmas season.

Easter

What do you think about when the Easter season comes each year? Do you think about Bunny Cottontail, with his colorful eggs, or the Easter Parade, with all its fancy floats? Those are not the real reason for having Easter. For Christians, Easter is a time that reminds us about Jesus the Christ who rose from the dead? It reminds us that there is a life after we leave earth and  that Jesus has prepared a wonderful life for us through what he did when God raised him from the dead. Without Jesus, Easter is not a real Christian holiday.

One of the things that has interested me as I have traveled to other parts of the world is the way other countries honor their past famous people. I remember

visiting the grave of an Indian ruler by the name of Shah Jahan. He built a fancy grave, named the Taj Mahal, which was built for his wife. It was so big that took nearly 20,000 men and 22 years to finish. It was called one of The Seven Wonders of the World.

On another trip, I visited one of the highest pyramids in Egypt, which was another grave for one of Egypt's kings. It was so large that it took thousands of slaves several years to make. It has been around many years and was probably there when Moses of the Bible was still in Egypt.

There is another grave that has more meaning for me than all the other ones in the world; it is the empty tomb of Jesus in the old city of Jerusalem. I can still see it in my mind! It was made by chipping rock out of the side

of a hill, and it belonged to a Jewish man by the name of Joseph of Arimathea. He allowed Jesus to be buried in it instead of himself. Jesus, who was the ever-living King of all Kings, did not need a fancy grave and he arose from the dead. His empty grave does not remind us of past kings, like the Taj Mahal and the Pyramids of Egypt. It reminds us about things in the future. On the first Easter morning, Jesus arose from the dead, leaving the empty grave behind. If we trust in Him and His way of Life, he tells us that we will also live beyond the grave. This is what Easter should mean to each of us!

Emmanuel Lighthouse Mission

The Emmanuel Lighthouse Mission, which name is often shortened to "ELM," is a place started by Emmanuel Baptist Church of Bryan, Texas to help people in need. The ELM office and buildings are located on  the property of Emmanuel Baptist Church, and the mission has been a part of Emmanuel Baptist Church for over 35 years.

The buildings used by ELM were first just two Air Force

barracks buildings that were gotten from an old military base that once was located in Bryan. They were placed across the street from the other church buildings. For a time, one of the buildings was used as a Coffee House and meeting place for the young people of the church, and the other building was used for Sunday school rooms.

About the year 1975, both of those buildings were no longer in use, and a church member by the name of Dayton Phillips was given permission to convert one of the buildings into a temporary place to live. Sometime after the building was made into a living space, there became a great need by refugees of many foreign countries to have a home.

So, about that time, the Emmanuel Baptist Church began

to sponsor refugees, and both buildings were used as living spaces. Over several years, there were refugees from Viet Nam, China, Cuba, and other places that made use of the ELM buildings.

Another part of the ELM ministry was to spread the gospel of Jesus, and a number of the refugees were Christians who later moved to other places

and were ministers of the gospel.

For a time, the two converted barracks were separated into one building for men and the other for women; but about 1990, there was a change to accept only women, and instead of inviting refugees, the people in the buildings were from the local area.

There have been a lot of changes over the years. The ministry began as a shelter with no kitchen and no rules. If the people were hungry, they were provided them with beans and rice. Many would stay up late at night and then sleep most of the next morning. We saw that we had problems. We put smoke detectors in the building, but some of the batteries ended up in their radios. So, we decided to make some rules, such as setting a curfew, requiring them to get a job, to attend church, and to work in the church garden on

Saturday mornings, to name a few of the rules. The people in the shelter were also given kitchen privileges in the church building and later there were facilities built into the shelter buildings.

The ELM shelter that began as two barracks buildings has now changed to one brick covered residence, and another nice building that is in the

process of being built. The people of the area and our Lord Jesus have been generous in supplying the needs of ELM in many ways.

Over the years, the ELM shelter has been run with the help of godly women directors and a council of men and women from the Bryan area. God has helped ELM provide for those who are in need, and the ministry has been able to share Jesus with those who come our way. God has given us a love for all who come to stay with us, and we pray that the time with us will be of great, lasting value to them.

Misawa, Japan

One of the hardest things I can remember ever doing was to leave Texas to go to Misawa, Japan. At that time, I was a chaplain in the United States Air Force, and I was given a new job at a military base in Japan. I had to leave my wife and four children, with the youngest still a baby.

As I left Texas early one morning in July 1959, I was saddened by having to leave my wife,

LaRue, and our family behind even though they would later follow me to Japan. I had never heard of Misawa, Japan, which is where I was headed. It was a strange feeling to be going to a country we had recently been at war with and to a place where I did not yet know any other Americans. I didn't have any choice in the matter, because my

boss, the USAF, said I had to go. I drove my car to San Francisco, California, and then I flew by airplane to Misawa Air Base, Japan.

At an earlier time in 1955, while I was then with the military in Hawaii, I had gone to Japan for a few days on a personal trip. The chaplain at the Air Force Base where I was visiting in Japan at that time invited me to preach in the Base Chapel, and I was delighted to do so. I do not remember all that I said, but I do remember trying to encourage the military people at church that day to witness to the Japanese people. They had maids in their homes, and they had many chances to speak to them and to others in their place of work about their faith in Jesus.

When I finally arrived at Misawa Air Base in 1959, one of the first things I learned was that some of the military people there were eager about starting a Christian church in the city of Misawa just outside of the air

base. On my first Sunday at Misawa Air Base, I was told about a group of airmen who were having a Baptist church service in a school building on the base. So, I went to their worship service. During the service, songbooks were passed out from a wooden footlocker with printing on the outside in large bold letters that said, "The First Baptist Church," and all the songbooks also said "The First Baptist Church" on their covers. I was excited to hear that there was the First Baptist Church in

Misawa City, So I asked a man by the name of Sgt. Doyle to tell me more about it. He just smiled and said it was not quite there yet, because it had not been built yet.

I was surprised that he would believe that they would one day have such a church in the city, but at that time all they had for it was a name. It was not there then, but it is today. The final name was not "The First Baptist," but it was later named "Misawa Baptist Church."

I was happy to be a part in starting the new church, but it did not happen right away. There were a number of people who became longtime friends as a result of the efforts to build the church. One of those men was Chaplain Coggins, another Baptist chaplain at Misawa Air Base, who helped to move the church service that began in the school to the base chapel for Friday services. There was an

airman by the name of Ron Williams, who was a member of

a church by the name of the Four Square Church, who was our song leader even though he was not a Baptist. We also had special meetings in our homes to continue the Christian work with the Japanese people.

Perhaps, the person who was the most important person in helping to start the Misawa Baptist Church was a Japanese man by the name of Junichi Ishikawa, known to everyone as "Johnny." His job was the interpreter for all the chaplains of Misawa Air Base, because he spoke well in both Japanese and English. Being also a Christian, Johnny helped to communicate between the Japanese and American people who were working on the new church. He helped in almost everything

from working with English classes for the high school students to the purchasing of land for a new building and the entire church building project.

Another person who was a big help was a Japanese man by the name of Hiroshi Suzuki. We met Hiroshi after he first contacted the commander of the air base about wanting to meet with some natives of America who spoke English. He had become interested in meeting Americans after he had been

listening to the "Voice of America" on the radio. The commanding general of the base asked the chaplain in charge of the Base Chapel if any of the chaplains there would like to take this young man for the summer. At one point the Staff Chaplain asked me if I would be interested. After I checked with my wife, LaRue, I told him we would be glad to take him. That was the beginning of a wonderful friendship between Hiroshi, who we called "Hero," and the Wilton family.

We had a wonderful time with Hero. He had the good manners and politeness common for the Japanese people. I remember that when Hero first came into our home, I offered to give him some of the buttermilk that I was drinking, because I liked it so much and never even thought anyone else might not like it. Hero was one of those persons who was not eager to drink buttermilk, and although he was polite about it, he was greatly relieved when he found out that it  was not necessary for him to drink buttermilk.

Hero's main interest in visiting with Americans was that he wanted to learn English better, but he was also ready to help anyone wanting to learn Japanese. We learned many things from Hero about Japan, and he was delighted to do anything we needed for him to do.

Although Hero was more interested in learning English, I was interested in introducing him to Jesus. So, I had the perfect project. At the time, I was teaching the Bible book of Matthew to Japanese young people and Johnny was helping to interpret between English and Japanese. Since the book would be learned better if we had the

text in Japanese, I gave Hero the job of translating the book of Matthew from English to Japanese. Hero did a great job, and we all had great fellowship.

When the time came to build the church in Misawa City, it first started as a Japanese mission connected with the Tokyo Baptist Church. It was an 8-hour train ride from Tokyo to Misawa, but with the help of the pastor of the Tokyo Baptist Church, Milton DuPriest, the mission was built and it later became the Misawa Baptist Church.

Today, there are actually two churches in Misawa City that

have resulted from the Misawa Baptist Mission. There is the Misawa Baptist Church, with

Japanese members, and there is also the Calvary Baptist Church, which is for English-speaking people.

Johnny, who was so helpful in getting the church started at Misawa, later became a part-time preacher, and he made a preaching tour in the USA.

While I was located at Killeen, Texas, he came and preached to our church, the Skyline Baptist Church.

In June 1991, Johnny also invited me to visit with him in Japan. Fawncyne, our older daughter, and I visited Johnny in Tokyo, Japan, where he then lived. From there, we also visited other friends in Japan, and we spent some time at Misawa City, where we attended services at the Misawa Baptist Church.

Sometime after Hero left us at Misawa, he became a Christian, and he also made a trip to Texas. He wanted me to baptize him, and I had the privilege of baptizing him into the fellowship of the Skyline Baptist Church in Killeen, Texas.

For awhile, he was also a student at Howard Payne University in Texas, and he later went to New

York, where he became the pastor of a Japanese church located there. Hero is now a Christian counselor in New York. His friendship has been a blessing to me over the years, and we still keep in contact.

Japan is a great nation with lovely people. It was great to

serve as a chaplain in the USAF and to have the privilege of ministering to the military personnel and making friends with many Japanese people. Thank-you Lord for being so good to me!

The Garden

I grew up on a farm, and we always had a garden. My mother was a great gardener. She would grow such things as beans, English peas, black-eyed  peas, onions, collard greens, beets, and many other vegetables. But to go along with the good vegetables, we also had a variety of weeds that came up. When the ground was wet, the weeds could be easily pulled up. My mother often sent me to the garden to pull weeds. That was a job I never liked.

We always had plenty to eat, even during hard times. Uncle Bob, my mother's brother, lived with us during some of the hard times. We usually had plenty of Black-eyed peas and other vegetables to eat. I remember that our favorite thing to eat was buttermilk with cornbread and

onions. I still remember Uncle Bob with his big bowl of buttermilk and cornbread. For him that was a full meal, and he had no complaints about the food.

The Bible tells us about three gardens: the Garden of Eden, the Garden of Gethsemane, and the Garden of Paradise. The first garden, The Garden of Eden, was the home of the first man and woman, Adam & Eve. They were put in the garden to care for it. The second garden, the Garden of Gethsemane, was the place where Jesus prayed before he went to the cross. The third garden, the Garden of Paradise, is where God's people will live in their future home in heaven. So, the garden is a very important place.

For many years, the women's shelter at Emmanuel Baptist Church has had a garden on the church property. The ladies who live in the shelter work in the garden on Saturday mornings, unless they have jobs that interfere with that work. We

have also given other people in the community the chance to use part of the shelter garden for their own personal use. One of our neighbors who lived close to the garden was named Beulah Brown. She was one of our best gardeners. One year, she grew more broccoli than we needed, and she had other vegetables to go with it.

Our shelter garden has grown large crops of tomatoes, sugar snap peas, okra, and other vegetables. We have been able to grow plants throughout the year, because some vegetables like cold weather, and other vegetables like hot weather. However, the most effort has been to grow vegetables for the Spring garden and the Fall garden.

It is exciting to see things grow, especially those things that we can eat. We put the seed in the ground, and God causes it to grow. It can be a happy time to watch as God does his miracle of growth and as we get the benefit of what he has provided.

India

I have had the chance to visit in India twice in my lifetime, and there are many interesting things and places to see there. India is the second largest nation in the world, and it has gone through many good times and many bad times. In the past, India has been ruled by those who have conquered the country and ruled over it, but today India is ruled by its own people.

The first time I went to India was in 1955 while I was in the United States Air Force (USAF) as a Chaplain in Hawaii. At that time, I went on a tour of the area in USAF airplanes when space was available for me. At first, my plan was to stop for three days at a place called Delhi, India. But due to mechanical problems with the airplane, our flight was delayed, and I stayed there for 10 whole days.

Years later, while I was the pastor of the Emmanuel Baptist Church in Bryan, Texas, I took my second trip to India. On that occasion, I went to Ajmere, India for a Christian crusade, and that also lasted about 10 days. So, I have precious memories of those 20 days in India.

One of the places that I most remember about India was a place called the Taj Mahal. It is

the grave of the wife of one of India's rulers. It is not like the graves we are familiar with. This one is actually so large and fancy that it is called one of the wonders of the world. It is a building that sits on a marble platform, and parts of it are as high as about 240 feet. It took about 20,000 men to build it.

This grave was built by a ruler by the name of Shah Jahan, who made it for a wife that he loved very much. Her name was Mumtaz Mahal. During the 18 years they were married, she had 14 children, and she died immediately after the birth of their last child.

Shah Jahan planned to build another grave on the other side of the Jamuna River, but it was never built. One of the ruler's sons took over the country about that time and he put the Shah in prison in a place called Agra Fort, which was also on the other side of the Jamuna River. From this prison, Shah Jahan could see the Taj Mahal across the river using a large glass lens located at the fort, but he was never allowed to visit it again. When he died, he was buried beside his

wife in the Taj Mahal. I had the privilege of visiting both the Taj Mahal and the Agra Fort.

When I was on my second trip in India, in 1969, I went to Ajmere, India for a week-long Christian crusade. My friend and interpreter was Rev. S.K. Paul. When I first got off the train in Ajmere, I waited for a few minutes at the train station. While I was waiting, a pitiful woman with a little baby in her arms came to me for a handout. I really did not have much money, but I gave her a coin. Then, another woman with a

little baby appeared for a handout. I told Rev. Paul about it, and he said, "If you had given her money, a third one would have appeared." The message about me had already passed around to all those around her.

We had a great time with the church in India, and one day we took a trip to see some of Northern India. I remember that during that trip I was given a ride on an elephant for the first time.

Bro. Paul was also a great musician, who sang and played

the accordion, in addition to being a preacher. One of his great hopes was to get the Gospel message to the thousands of villages in his area of India. When the time came to return home, as I was leaving on the train, and as Rev. Paul walked by my window of the moving train, he told me that he needed an accordion for his Gospel ministry. After I returned home to Texas, the Emmanuel Baptist Church and I sent him that accordion. He was very grateful, and he sent us pictures of his work. He had a fine witness to the people of Northern India.

Another great memory of India was visiting the grave of Mahatma Gandhi in Delhi, India. He was one of the greatest of the leaders of men. He was unselfish and worked for the people of India to have freedom. It was through his leadership that India did receive her freedom.   His memorial was very simple, but I think his life,

compared with the life of Shah Jahan, was much greater, just like light is better than darkness. The brilliance of his influence will shine upon India for many years.

India has many good people today. My Indian friends have blessed me greatly, and I have many fond memories of my visits to India.

Why Me, Lord?

When I think about all the things that have happened to me and all that I have been able to do, I have to ask the question, "Why Me, Lord?" I am not the first person to ask that question, because it has been asked by people around the  world and throughout many years. As a matter of fact, even songs have been written on that subject.

When I think about when the Lord picked on me one day to become a preacher, I have to ask,

"Why Me, Lord?" I had other plans, even to be a big success, but I had no plans or desire to be a preacher.  Why, Lord, did you send me around the  world to preach your message, and to spend 3 years in Japan? Why did you pick on me to stay with the Emmanuel Baptist Church for 40 years, and why have you left  me here to enjoy the fellowship of your saints for so many years?

And when I think about the beautiful Christian lady that became my wife for almost 61 years and the four lovely children, the six grandchildren and the six great-grandchildren that have become a part of my life, I have to ask, "Why Me, Lord?"

And I have to ask "Why Me, Lord?" at least one more time. Why have you always been there for me when I needed you, even when it seemed like things were bad all around me? Really Lord, I have no clue as to why you should have picked on me so much?

After thinking again about all the wonderful ways the Lord has helped me, I have decided that the answer to the question, "Why me, Lord?", is not all that important. But thank you, Lord, for picking me! The journey has been wonderful and the memories have brought lasting happiness!

Picture Credits

—